EVERYONE LOVES

CHILDREN

"It's really cool—I can make whatever ⌐ ⌐⌐⌐⌐⌐. ⌐ ⌐⌐⌐⌐ ⌐ ⌐⌐⌐⌐⌐⌐ of *The Very Hungry Caterpillar!*"
—Child, 6 years old, showing off his ScratchJr book report

"I was really excited to show my dad my space project. I was really proud of the characters disappearing and showing up again."
—Second grader

"My favorite block is Repeat Forever. You can take the Move Left block and then if you put the red Repeat Forever block at the end of it, your car will move left and left and left . . . forever!"
—Kindergarten student

TEACHERS

"Students love exploring and discovering new blocks on their own, and I encourage the students to share these discoveries with their peers. I find that the best experience of the students is having them learn together."
—Kindergarten teacher

"One of our report card skills is 'child can follow multistep directions.' You can see the kids practicing this when they sequence their programs."
—Kindergarten teacher

"The students love working on ScratchJr, in and out of class. I like that they have to think in advance about what they are going to do and then test it throughout the process."
—First-grade teacher

"Technology is here now and it's the future, and I think the earlier that we can get kids into it, the better off they'll be . . . and it's fun. We all know that people learn when they're having fun."
—Second-grade teacher

PARENTS

"My daughter always thought that she wasn't as good with technology as her brother, but ScratchJr showed her how much she was capable of."
—Parent of a second grader and a kindergartner

"For skeptical parents out there, I would tell them to embrace technology and go for it with their kids. My daughter and I used ScratchJr at home and it was tremendous. We loved it."
—Parent of a five-year-old

"I am proud to support ScratchJr. My son is already playing it on his own, making the ducks do crazy things (he was inspired by one of the sample programs). He's just having simple fun with it now, and I am sure it is the best start for doing something deeper later."
—Parent of a five-year-old

"I'm treating ScratchJr as another language. I think of it as a constructive tool instead of a game tool; I think if other parents approach it that way, then their kids will get more out of it."
—Parent of a second grader

THE OFFICIAL

BOOK

THE OFFICIAL

SCRATCH jr

BOOK

Help your kids learn to code!

MARINA UMASCHI BERS AND MITCHEL RESNICK

NO STARCH PRESS
SAN FRANCISCO

THE OFFICIAL SCRATCHJR BOOK. Copyright © 2016 by Marina Umaschi Bers and Mitchel Resnick.

Printed in USA

First printing

19 18 17 16 15   1 2 3 4 5 6 7 8 9

Text stock is SFI certified

ISBN-10: 1-59327-671-0
ISBN-13: 978-1-59327-671-3

Publisher: William Pollock
Production Editor: Serena Yang
Cover and Interior Design: Beth Middleworth
Developmental Editors: Liz Chadwick and Tyler Ortman
Technical Reviewer: Claire Caine
Copyeditor: Rachel Monaghan
Compositor: Serena Yang
Proofreader: Lisa Devoto Farrell
Indexer: BIM Indexing & Proofreading Services

Hand illustration used under license from Shutterstock.com.

For information on distribution, translations, or bulk sales, please contact No Starch Press, Inc. directly:

No Starch Press, Inc.
245 8th Street, San Francisco, CA 94103
phone: 415.863.9900; info@nostarch.com
www.nostarch.com

Library of Congress Cataloging-in-Publication Data

Bers, Marina Umaschi, author.
  The official ScratchJr book : help your kids learn to code / by Marina Umaschi Bers and Mitchel Resnick.
      pages cm
  Includes index.
  Summary: "An introduction to coding for parents and kids. Includes 18 hands-on activities using ScratchJr, a programming language designed for young children (ages 5-7). Teaches computational thinking, literacy, and math skills through animated collages, interactive stories, and playable games"-- Provided by publisher.
  Includes bibliographical references and index.
  ISBN 978-1-59327-671-3 -- ISBN 1-59327-671-0
  1. Scratch (Computer program language) 2. Computer programming--Study and teaching (Elementary) 3. Computer programming--Computer-assisted instruction. I. Resnick, Mitchel, author. II. Title.
  QA76.73.S345B47 2016
  005.13'3071--dc23
                                2015030543

BRIEF CONTENTS

CONTENTS IN DETAIL

PREFACE

This book's history stretches back
50 years when, in the 1960s, Seymour
Papert presented a bold new vision of
how computers might enter the lives of
children. At the time, computers still cost
tens of thousands of dollars, if not more.
The first personal computers would not

become commercially available for another decade. But Seymour foresaw that computers would eventually become accessible for everyone, even children, and he lay the intellectual foundation for how computing could transform the ways children learn and play.

While other researchers imagined that computers might someday be used to deliver information to children or pose questions to children, Seymour had a very different vision. He believed that children should be in control of computers, using them to experiment, explore, and express themselves. Seymour and his colleagues at MIT developed the programming language Logo specifically for children so that children could program their own pictures, stories, and games. In his 1980 book *Mindstorms: Children, Computers, and Powerful Ideas*, Seymour argued that children should program computers, not the other way around.

The two of us writing this book (Marina and Mitch) worked closely with Seymour when we were graduate students at MIT, and we were deeply influenced by his ideas. Both of us have dedicated our careers to extending Seymour's work, providing young people with opportunities for designing, creating, and inventing with new technologies.

Mitch's Lifelong Kindergarten research group at the MIT Media Lab collaborated closely with the LEGO Group on the MINDSTORMS and WeDo robotics kits and cofounded the Computer Clubhouse Network of after-school learning centers for youth from low-income communities. More recently, the group developed the Scratch programming language and online community, which is used by millions of young people (ages 8 and up) around the world.

Marina's Developmental Technologies (DevTech) Research Group at the Eliot-Pearson Department of Child Study and Human Development at Tufts University has focused on early childhood learning, developing technologies and activities for preschool, kindergarten, and early elementary students. The group developed the ideas and prototypes that led to the KIBO robot kit, which enables young children (ages 4–7) to program robotic projects by putting together sequences of wooden blocks. With KIBO, children learn programming without screens or keyboards. In 2013 Marina co-founded KinderLab Robotics to make KIBO widely available. The ideas underlying Marina's and the DevTech Research Group's work are described in Marina's books *Blocks to Robots: Learning with Technology in the Early Childhood Classroom* (Teachers College Press, 2007) and *Designing Digital Experiences for Positive Youth Development: From Playpen to Playground* (Oxford University Press, 2012).

In 2010, Marina suggested that our two groups work together to develop a programming language for young children, extending MIT's work on Scratch and drawing on Tufts' experience with early childhood learning, and thus the idea for ScratchJr was born. We teamed up with Paula Bontá and Brian Silverman of the Playful Invention Company (PICO), who brought strong expertise in the design and development of programming languages for children (and who also had worked closely with Seymour Papert). ScratchJr has been a true team effort, with contributions by many people at Tufts, MIT, PICO, and elsewhere. We encourage you to look at the ScratchJr website (*http://www.scratchjr.org/*) for a full list of contributors.

We've been thrilled by the response to ScratchJr from thousands of children, parents, and teachers around the world, but we recognize that more and better support materials are needed to help people use ScratchJr to its full potential. We wrote this book to support the use of ScratchJr in both homes and schools. We hope that you find the book useful, and we look forward to hearing your feedback and suggestions.

We want to thank members of the ScratchJr team who helped in researching, writing, and producing this book, particularly Claire Caine, Amanda Strawhacker, Mollie Elkin, Dylan Portelance, Amanda Sullivan, and Alex Puganali.

We are also extremely grateful to Tyler Ortman and Serena Yang at our publisher, No Starch Press. They have provided invaluable help and advice throughout the process of writing and publishing the book.

ScratchJr would not have been possible without generous financial support from the National Science Foundation (grant number DRL-1118664) and the Scratch Foundation. If you enjoy this book and ScratchJr, we hope you'll consider making a donation to the Scratch Foundation (*http://www.scratchfoundation .org/*) to support the future development of ScratchJr software and educational materials.

Enjoy!

Marina and Mitch

AN INTRODUCTION TO SCRATCHJR

In recent years there has been a prolif-
eration of educational apps and games,
full of flashy graphics and engaging
music, for young children. But many of
these educational apps have been frustrating for parents and teachers. The

problem: very few educational apps provide young children with opportunities to design, create, and express themselves. That's what motivated us to create ScratchJr.

WHAT IS SCRATCHJR?

ScratchJr is an introductory programming language that encourages creativity and expression, enabling five- to seven-year-old children to create their own interactive projects through *coding*, as it is often called these days.

Using ScratchJr, children can snap together programming blocks to make characters move, jump, dance, and sing. They can modify how their characters look, design their own backgrounds, add their own voices and sounds and even photos of themselves—and then use the programming blocks to bring their characters to life.

ScratchJr was inspired by the popular Scratch programming language, used by millions of young people (ages eight and up) around the world. We redesigned the interface and programming language to make it developmentally appropriate, as well as fun and engaging, for younger children.

Based on feedback from children, parents, and teachers, we went through dozens of prototypes for ScratchJr to make it as effective as possible for its purpose. We hope that you find it a useful tool for engaging children.

WHY DID WE CREATE SCRATCHJR?

We believe that every child should be given the opportunity to learn how to code. Coding is often seen as difficult or exclusive, but we see it as a new type of literacy—a skill that should be accessible for everyone. Coding helps learners to organize their thinking and express their ideas, just as writing does.

As young children code with ScratchJr, they learn how to create and express themselves with the computer, rather than just interact with software created by others. Children learn to think sequentially, explore cause and effect, and develop design and problem-solving skills. At the same time, they learn to use math and language in a meaningful and motivating context.

As children use ScratchJr, they aren't just learning to code, they are coding to learn.

WHO IS THIS BOOK FOR?

This book is for anyone who wants to help children learn to code and, more broadly, to think creatively and reason systematically. It was written particularly for people without coding experience or technical expertise, but it can also be helpful for those who do have expertise but don't have experience working with young children.

ScratchJr was designed especially for five- to seven-year-olds as a precursor to other programming languages. With a little additional support, younger children can enjoy it too, and it can also be useful for introducing older children to coding before they move on to other programming languages (like Scratch).

And, of course, for parents or educators without any coding knowledge, this book is a good way to learn the basics of coding. The best way to learn something new is to teach it to someone else. So as you help young children learn to code, you'll be learning too.

WHAT DO YOU NEED?

You need to have ScratchJr downloaded on a tablet. ScratchJr is available free of charge and runs on iOS and Android devices. There are links to download ScratchJr at *http://www.scratchjr.org/*. You can download it from the App Store for an iPad, and it runs on second-generation or newer iPads. Download it from the Google Play Store if you have a 7-inch Android tablet or larger that runs Android 4.2 (Kit Kat) or later.

WHAT'S IN THIS BOOK?

This book consists of four chapters. Chapter 1 introduces some initial activities to familiarize you with the basic features of ScratchJr. The rest of the book assumes you can make your way around ScratchJr, so don't skip the first chapter! The remaining chapters describe projects that young children can create with ScratchJr. Chapter 2 shows playful animations, Chapter 3 shows how to tell interactive stories, and Chapter 4 shows how to create fun games.

Each chapter is made up of a set of short activities that introduce new programming blocks and features and a final project to integrate all of this knowledge. Each activity reinforces age-appropriate math and literacy skills, and includes tips and challenges for children who want to explore more.

Finally, the appendices have resources and references to help you make the best use of ScratchJr.

HOW SHOULD YOU USE THIS BOOK?

We developed the projects as a sequence of activities that will incrementally teach different aspects of ScratchJr in a developmentally appropriate way. But don't feel as though you need to follow this book step-by-step. Feel free to mix and match and adapt our suggested projects to your own and your child's interests. Follow your child's lead. Every detour is a child-directed learning experience. ScratchJr is a tool for self-expression. Children should feel free to explore ScratchJr's many buttons and features and to use characters and backgrounds that are meaningful to them. This is something we hear frequently from parents and teachers.

And please, do let us know how it's going! Hearing about all the different ways you've used this book will help us to improve ScratchJr further. Send your comments to *info@scratchjr.org*.

Have fun!

CHAPTER 1
GETTING STARTED

Welcome to ScratchJr! The projects that you can make with ScratchJr are limited only by your imagination. If you can dream it, you can make it.

This chapter will teach you the basics of using ScratchJr, and together we'll make a dance party! You'll learn how to make characters move and speak, how to change the background, and how to save your work so you can build on it again or share it with your friends. You'll also learn how to delete objects and undo steps.

After finishing this chapter, you'll know your way around the ScratchJr interface, and you'll know how to use the programming blocks to bring your characters to life.

ACTIVITY 1: THROW A DANCE PARTY!

Let's get the ScratchJr cat to dance with a friend on a stage.

This chapter will show you how to set up and complete your first project.

STEP 1: OPEN THE APP

This is the first screen you'll see when you open the ScratchJr app. Tap the **Home** button on the left.

STEP 2: MAKE A NEW PROJECT

The home screen shows all of your saved ScratchJr projects. In the following picture, you can see two projects that have already been created. If this is your first project, you'll see only the plus sign. Tap the plus sign to make a new project.

STEP 3: MAKE THE CAT MOVE!

This is where the magic happens! You can make amazing animations, silly stories, and great games—all from the ScratchJr editor. Whatever you make will play in the center of the screen. We call this area the *stage*.

Each new project starts with the ScratchJr cat. To make the cat move, we can use the *motion blocks*, which are in the blue *palette* of programming blocks. Use your finger to drag one of the blue arrow blocks to the *programming area*.

Tap the blue block, and the cat moves in the direction of the arrow!

You can drag more blocks to the programming area and snap them together to make a sequence of actions, which we call a *script*.

Add some more blue motion blocks to make the cat dance. Can you guess what movement each block makes? Experiment to see which blocks make the best dance.

To run the script and see the cat dance, tap any of the blocks in the script. Notice that the script runs from the beginning no matter which block you tap, and each block is highlighted as it runs.

Congratulations! You just made your first computer program! Now let's turn it into a dance party!

STEP 4: USE THE GREEN FLAG

There are other ways to make your project run besides tapping on scripts. You can also use the Start on Green Flag block to start your script.

First, tap the yellow button in the *block categories area* to show the *triggering blocks*. Select the **Start on Green Flag** block, drag it to the programming area, and snap it onto the front of your script.

Now tap the **Green Flag** button at the top of the screen.

The cat will dance just like it did when you tapped on the script!

You can see that there are other triggering blocks. You'll find out how to use these as you go through the other projects in this book.

STEP 5: ADD A BACKGROUND

Let's get the cat to dance on a stage, instead of just a plain white background. Select a new background by tapping on the button with the blue sky and green grass at the top of the main screen. This is called the *Change Background button*.

You'll see loads of backgrounds that you can choose from. For our dancing cat, let's choose the theatre. Tap the check mark at the top to load it into your stage.

Congratulations! Your cat is a star!

The cat is smiling and dancing, but it looks a bit lonely dancing on its own. . . .

STEP 6: ADD ANOTHER CHARACTER

Let's give your cat a friend. Tap the plus sign on the left side of your screen to add a character.

If you scroll down the page, you'll see the many characters you can choose from. Tap the character you want to add, and then tap the check mark to add it to your project. We've chosen the penguin.

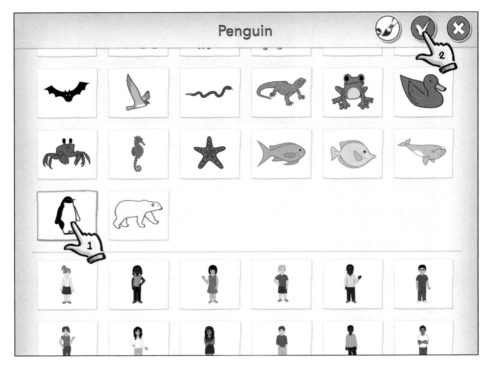

Now there are two characters on the stage. To the left of the stage is the *character area*, which shows you all the characters involved in your project.

The new character will always appear in the middle of the stage. To move the character, use your finger to drag it wherever you want on the stage. We've dragged each of our characters to a spotlight.

You might notice that the script you wrote for the cat disappeared after you selected a new character. Don't worry: the script is still there! It's in the cat's programming area, and now the screen is showing the programming area for the penguin. Each character has its own scripts, like actors in a play. To see the cat's script, tap the cat in the character area on the left, and you'll see that your script is still there. Then select the penguin again so that you can give it dance moves of its own.

STEP 7: DON'T JUST DANCE, SAY SOMETHING!

Let's make the penguin say something before it dances. You can add speech bubbles for characters using the purple Say block. Tap the purple button in the block categories area to reveal the *looks blocks.*

Drag the **Say** block to the programming area.

Let's change the text of the Say block from "hi" to "Let's dance!" First, tap the word *hi* to make the keyboard appear. Use the backspace key to delete *hi*, and then type **Let's dance!** or whatever you want the penguin to say.

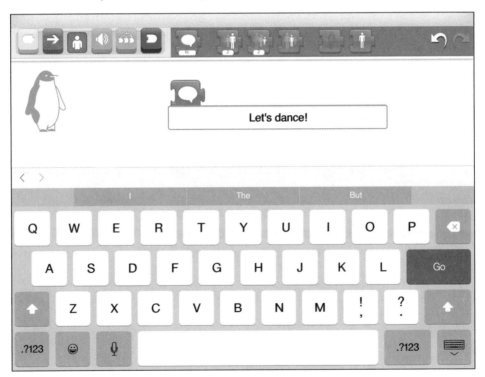

Add some blue motion blocks to make the penguin dance, and then put a **Start on Green Flag** block at the beginning of the penguin's script.

Now try it out by tapping the **Green Flag** button ( ) at the top of the screen.

You'll see that the scripts for the cat and the penguin start running at the same time. When you tap the Green Flag button, it will run every script that begins with a Start on Green Flag block for every character, all at the same time. This will be really useful as you make bigger projects with more characters.

STEP 8: ADD A TITLE

You can display a title on the stage by tapping the **Add Text** button ( ) at the top of the screen. In the window that pops up, type **Dance Party**.

You can drag the title around the screen and place it anywhere you want.

You can also use the **Change Size** ( ) and **Change Color** ( ) buttons to change the size and color of the title you give your project. Play around and see what suits your stage best. Press **Go** to try it out on the stage. If you want to edit the title again, you can tap on the words to bring the text window back up.

STEP 9: NAME YOUR PROJECT

Now give your project a name so that when you open ScratchJr again and see your projects on the home screen, you'll know which project is which.

To name your project, tap the yellow tab in the top-right corner of the screen. Then delete the current project name (*Project 1*) and type **Dance Party**. When you're ready to return to the main screen, tap the check mark.

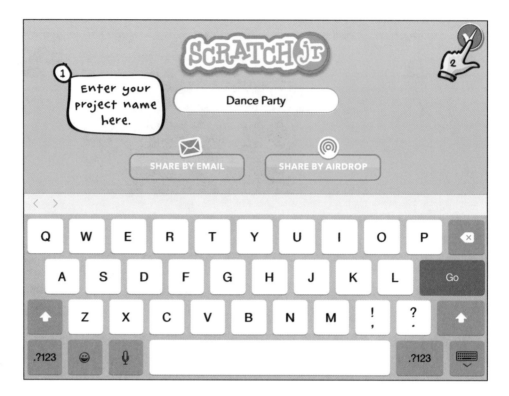

If you want to send your project to someone else who has ScratchJr, you can do that from this screen too. For more details on how to share your projects, see the Frequently Asked Questions on the ScratchJr website (*http://www.scratchjr.org/about .html#faq*).

You're almost finished, but you have one important step left!

STEP 10: SAVE YOUR PROJECT

To save your project and go back to the home screen, tap the **Home** button (🏠) in the top-left corner. Your project will not be saved until you return to the home screen, so it's a good idea to do this a few times while you are working on your project so that you don't lose anything.

To continue working on your project, just tap the small image of the project on the home screen. This will take you back to the ScratchJr editor for that project.

HINTS

The ScratchJr characters are all either facing forward or facing right when you first add them to your stage. If you want a character to face to the left, drag a Move Left block to the programming area and tap the block.

The character will turn to the left and take a step. You can then delete this block and the character will continue to face left.

TIPS FOR GROWN-UPS

ScratchJr makes different sounds when you perform different actions on the interface. These sounds can be very useful when you first start using ScratchJr. For example, when you have successfully snapped blocks together in a script, you'll hear a "pop." If you want to turn the sounds off, however, you can just turn the volume off on your device.

DON'T BE AFRAID TO EXPLORE!

As you explore the various features of ScratchJr, you should feel free to experiment, try new features, and test out new blocks. You can make your project whatever you want it to be in many ways: you could move your party to the beach, put a boat in the background, add more characters, or do almost anything else you want to do. A good feature of ScratchJr is that if you decide you don't like any of the changes you've made, you can easily get rid of them.

We'll show you some simple ways to do this.

UNDOING AND REDOING

You can undo your most recent actions by tapping the Undo button at the far end of the blocks palette. If you tap the Undo button multiple times, you will undo more and more of your work, one step at a time.

If you've undone several steps, the Redo button will reverse the most recent Undo.

DELETING OBJECTS

To delete something from ScratchJr, press it with your finger and hold it for a few seconds (sometimes called a *long press*) until you see a red X appear on the object. Tap the X to delete the object.

You can use this process to delete a character within a project or even delete an entire project from the home screen.

DELETING BLOCKS

To get rid of a block or even a whole script from the programming area, just drag it back up to the blocks palette and let go. You can have any color palette showing to do this; the palette doesn't have to be the same color as the blocks you are deleting.

A GUIDED TOUR OF THE SCRATCHJR INTERFACE

Now that you have a good grasp of the basics, you can take a look at all the buttons and features. Try a few of the ones we skipped earlier. If you feel overwhelmed, don't worry: the rest of the book's projects will show you how to use everything! It's okay to skip ahead and refer back here when you need to.

Let's start with the buttons at the top of the editor.

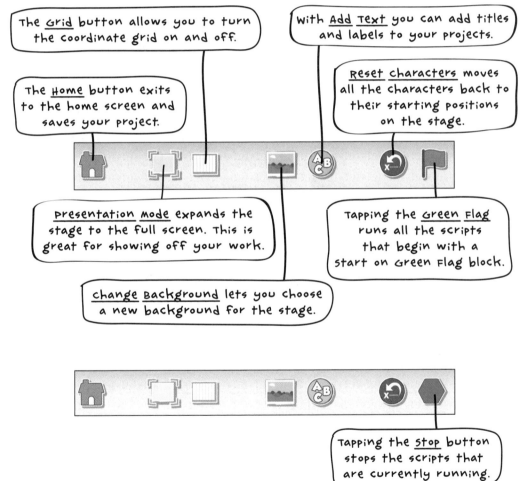

The Grid button allows you to turn the coordinate grid on and off.

With Add Text you can add titles and labels to your projects.

The Home button exits to the home screen and saves your project.

Reset characters moves all the characters back to their starting positions on the stage.

Presentation Mode expands the stage to the full screen. This is great for showing off your work.

Tapping the Green Flag runs all the scripts that begin with a start on Green Flag block.

Change Background lets you choose a new background for the stage.

Tapping the Stop button stops the scripts that are currently running.

In the character area, you can select among the characters in your project to give them scripts or tap the plus sign to add a new character. Tap the name to rename a character, or tap the paintbrush to edit its image. To delete a character, press and hold it until you see the red X; then tap the X.

Using Project Information, you can change the title of your project and share the project with friends.

The pages area allows you to select among the pages in your project. Check out "Turn the Page!" on page 58 to see how to use the pages area.

The block categories area is where you select a category of programming blocks: triggering, motion, looks, sound, control, or end.

The blocks palette displays blocks you can add to your project.

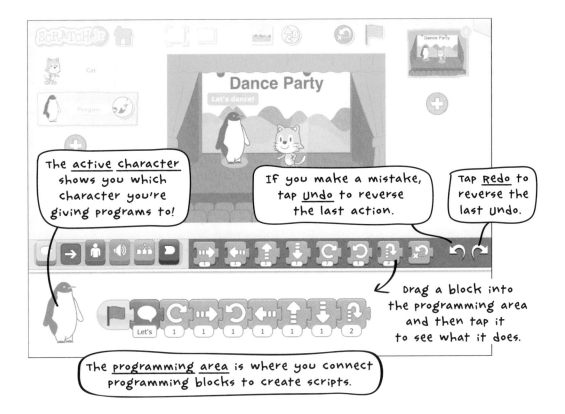

The active character shows you which character you're giving programs to!

If you make a mistake, tap Undo to reverse the last action.

Tap Redo to reverse the last Undo.

Drag a block into the programming area and then tap it to see what it does.

The programming area is where you connect programming blocks to create scripts.

WHAT'S NEXT?

You now have a good working knowledge of the ScratchJr interface. Move on to the next chapter to learn about new programming blocks and to explore new types of projects.

CHAPTER 2
ANIMATIONS

Let's get more familiar with ScratchJr by creating some simple animations. To get your characters moving, you just need to give them scripts that describe how you want them to move.

We'll do four small activities together, and then we'll make a final animation at the end of the chapter!

ACTIVITY 2: MAKE YOUR CAT MOVE!

Can you get the ScratchJr cat to move from one side of the screen to the other? Figure out how many Move Right blocks you need!

WHAT YOU'LL LEARN

In this activity, you will explore some options for making the cat move on the screen. All motion in ScratchJr follows a grid, and you'll discover how to change the number of steps along this grid using the motion blocks.

You'll also learn how to use the Start on Green Flag block to reset your cat's position so that you can run your script again and again.

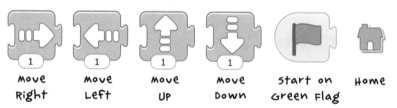

| Move Right | Move Left | Move Up | Move Down | Start on Green Flag | Home |

HOW TO MAKE IT

You can make a very simple script with lots of Move Right blocks, and the cat will take one step to the right for each block. But isn't it a lot of work to drag and connect all these motion blocks together?

There must be a better way to do this. . . .

Aha! There is a number at the bottom of each motion block. Let's see what happens when you change it.

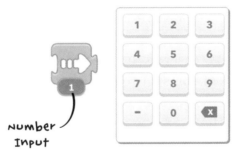

Number
Input

When you tap the number at the bottom of the motion block, a keypad appears on the right side of the programming area. Enter a new number with the keypad, and then tap the block. Notice how far the cat moves with just one programming block.

Let's explore the meaning of this number a little more.

1. Tap the **Grid** button at the top of the screen to show the grid.

You will see a grid appear on the stage. This grid will help you keep track of where your characters are on the stage.

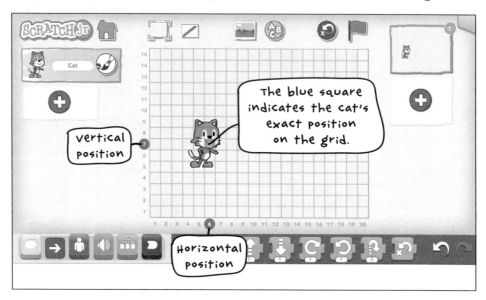

2. Now tap your script again. See what happens when the cat moves from one spot to another on the stage? The blue square will move with your cat, and the blue numbered circles will indicate the cat's new position on the stage.

3. Try to make your cat visit every corner of the stage by using the first four motion blocks in the blue blocks palette.

4. If you start your script with a **Start on Green Flag** block and you run the script by tapping the Green Flag button at the top of the screen, the cat will reset itself to its starting position before the script runs.

This will make it easier for you to make changes in your script and retest it, since the cat will always start from the same location. You can change the cat's starting position by dragging the cat to another location on the stage.

5. When you are finished having the cat visit all four corners of the stage, save your project by tapping the **Home** button (). You'll return to the home screen, where you can access all of your projects and make new ones.

HINTS

There is no block for diagonal movement in ScratchJr. If you want to move the cat to a corner of the screen, you will have to move it to that spot with motion blocks for horizontal steps and vertical steps.

LOOKING FOR A CHALLENGE?

If you have multiple motion blocks of the same kind in a row, see if you can simplify your script by changing the number input.

Experiment with the Hop block and see what happens when you change the number input.

Notice that changing the number input to 4 will not have the same effect as putting two Hop blocks next to each other.

This is because the number input on a Hop block controls how high a character will hop, not how many times a character will hop.

MAKING CONNECTIONS

LITERACY CONNECTION: SPELLING A NAME

Now that you've programmed your cat to move, come up with a name for the cat! Tap the **Paintbrush** button to go to the paint editor, and replace the word *Cat* at the top with your cat's name. Think about how each letter sounds as you try to spell it.

MATH CONNECTION:
SEEING HOW MANY WAYS YOU CAN GET TO 10

See if you can calculate which number on the grid the cat will end up on after you run your script. How many different scripts can you create that will make the cat move to that particular location?

Hint: there are many different ways to write a script and get to 10! Play around with changing the number inputs for the motion blocks to see what happens.

TIPS FOR GROWN-UPS

Children may have trouble understanding that one motion block can be used to make a character move several steps. Try setting up these two scripts to show how they make a character move the same distance.

ACTIVITY 3: MAKE YOUR CAT TURN!

Next, you'll make your cat turn right (clockwise) or left (counter-clockwise).

WHAT YOU'LL LEARN

In this activity, you'll create another new project and learn how to use the Turn Right and Turn Left blocks to tilt your cat clockwise or counterclockwise. See how many times your cat has to turn right or left to make a full circle. Then try thinking of other ways you could use these blocks!

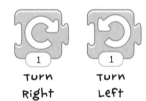

Turn Right   Turn Left

HOW TO MAKE IT

1. From the home screen, tap the plus sign to make a new project.

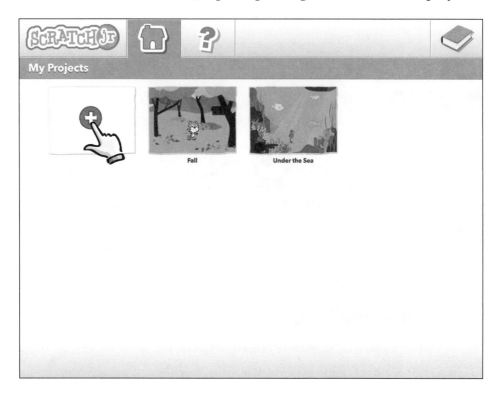

2. Drag the **Turn Right** block from the blue blocks palette to the programming area.

3. Change the number input, and tap the **Turn Right** block to see how the cat responds.

    Experiment to figure out what number will make the cat turn upside down. Then figure out what the number should be to make the cat turn a full circle.

4. Don't forget to start your script with a **Start on Green Flag** block so that the cat returns to a vertical position before turning.

5. Now try the same thing with the **Turn Left** block!

HINTS

Notice that you can drag the cat around on the screen with your finger, and this will reset the cat's starting position. You can't rotate the cat with your finger, though! You have to use a motion block to do that.

LOOKING FOR A CHALLENGE?

See whether you can make the cat do a cartwheel by making it turn and move forward *at the same time*.

    Hint: use two scripts for this and start both scripts at the same time with a Start on Green Flag block. You can also use this trick with Move Right and Move Up blocks to make the cat move diagonally!

MAKING CONNECTIONS

LITERACY CONNECTION: DESCRIBING FEELINGS

Think of a story about why your cat is spinning. Is the cat happy? Sad? Dizzy? Explain your project to a friend, and make sure they understand why your cat is feeling that way.

MATH CONNECTION: TELLING TIME

Think of how a clock's hands move around its face, and compare that direction to the direction of the cat when it turns. Which one of the turn blocks—Turn Left or Turn Right—moves the cat in the same direction as a clock's hands?

See how many times the cat has to turn to go a quarter of the way around a circle. If you double the number input, will the cat turn halfway around the circle?

TIPS FOR GROWN-UPS

You can think of the Turn Right and Turn Left blocks in terms of a clock face. Each turn moves the cat "one hour"—that is, one-twelfth of the full circle.

ACTIVITY 4: LET'S PLAY HIDE-AND-SEEK!

The cat in this activity is playing a game of hide-and-seek. The cat will disappear and then reappear three times.

WHAT YOU'LL LEARN

In Chapter 1, you used a purple block to make a character say something. In this activity, you will learn how to use the purple Hide and Show blocks to make the cat disappear and reappear.

HOW TO MAKE IT

1. First, select the purple category of blocks—the looks blocks. These control how a character looks.

2. Drag the **Hide** and **Show** blocks to the programming area, but don't snap them together yet. Tap the **Hide** block to see what happens. Now tap the **Show** block. These blocks make a character disappear and reappear.

3. Now drag two more sets of **Hide** and **Show** blocks to the programming area, and snap them onto the first set to make a script that causes the cat to disappear and then reappear three times.

4. Tap the script to see how your cat plays hide-and-seek.

HINTS

If you combine motion blocks with the Hide and Show blocks, you will see that your cat can still move even when it's hidden!

LOOKING FOR A CHALLENGE?

Try to make your cat disappear and then reappear at another place on the screen. Can you make your cat disappear and then reappear twice, each time moving to a new place on the screen? How about three times?

Try out other purple looks blocks, such as Grow and Shrink, to see how they change your cat's appearance.

Grow   Shrink

How large can you make the cat? How small can you make it? Notice what happens when you change the number input on these blocks. See if you can get the cat back to its original size. See whether the Start on Green Flag block has any effect on the cat's size.

MAKING CONNECTIONS

LITERACY CONNECTION: TELLING A STORY

Why does your cat keep disappearing? Think of a story about why your cat is disappearing and reappearing, and share this story with a friend. Remember to speak clearly and explain what is happening in your scripts to help you tell the story!

MATH CONNECTION: OBSERVING AND COUNTING

Count the number of times your cat disappears and how many times it reappears. Does this match the number of blocks you used?

TIPS FOR GROWN-UPS

It is helpful to have a conversation about what happens when you place a programming block after the Hide block. Sometimes children have trouble understanding why they cannot see their character complete a script after it has disappeared.

Notice that a Start on Green Flag block will reset a character's position, but it will not make a hidden character visible.

ACTiViTY 5: DO SOMETHING OVER AND OVER!

In this activity, you'll make your cat repeat multiple actions on the stage without using multiple blocks of the same kind.

WHAT YOU'LL LEARN

Until now, if you wanted to repeat an action, you had to use several blocks of the same kind or change the number input on a block.

In this activity, you'll learn how to use the Repeat block and the Repeat Forever block to repeat one or more actions.

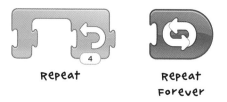

Repeat   Repeat Forever

HOW TO MAKE IT

Let's take a look at your script from the previous activity:

The first two blocks (the Hide block and the Show block) make the cat disappear and reappear. This pattern of Hide and Show blocks is then repeated two more times. But rather than use all of these blocks, you can use a Repeat block to make the first pattern run several times.

1. First, delete the last four blocks of the script by dragging them back to the blocks palette. You are left with only a single Hide block and a single Show block.

2. Now, tap the orange category of blocks to reveal the *control blocks*.

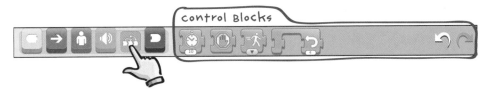

3. Drag the **Repeat** block to the programming area and position it around the two purple looks blocks.

   You can change the number in the bubble of the Repeat block to whatever you want. If you want the script to do exactly what it did in the previous activity, you would change this number to 3.

   You can use a big number to make your cat disappear and reappear many times, but what if you want the cat to disappear and reappear forever? Then, instead of using a Repeat block, you could end your script with the Repeat Forever block. Try it! (To stop a repeating script, tap the red stop sign button that replaces the green flag button while a script is running.)

HINTS

You can drag multiple blocks around the programming area at the same time. To delete four of the six Hide and Show blocks from your previous script in one motion, just put your finger on the third block and drag it back to the blocks palette. All of the blocks to the right of that block will move with it.

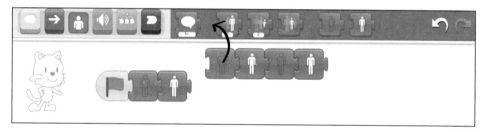

LOOKING FOR A CHALLENGE?

Put other blocks inside and outside of the Repeat block. Try out some motion blocks from the blue category. Notice how the animation changes depending on whether a block is or is not included in the Repeat block.

You could also have a Repeat block within a script that ends with a Repeat Forever block. Try it! The entire script will repeat forever, and each time it repeats, the blocks inside the Repeat block will repeat for the number of times specified by the number input.

MAKING CONNECTIONS

LITERACY CONNECTION: COMPARING YOUR SCRIPTS TO SENTENCES

As your cat moves on the stage, you will see that the blocks in your scripts light up one at a time, starting at the left end of the script and ending at the right end of the script. The blocks light up from left to right because ScratchJr reads your script in the same way you read sentences in a book! Some blocks take longer to run than others, a bit like how some words take longer to say.

TIPS FOR GROWN-UPS

Point out to children that they can follow the flow of a script by looking at the blocks in the programming area while the script is running. The blocks will become a darker shade of their color when they are running. In this picture, the Show block is a darker shade of purple, which means it is currently running.

The next time you run a ScratchJr script, watch closely and you'll see how the program runs. Seeing the exact action each block performs is one of the advantages of playing a script in the main interface rather than in Presentation Mode.

MATH CONNECTION: COMPARING TWO SCRIPTS

Make a script that uses the Repeat block, and make another script that does the same thing but does not use the Repeat block. Compare the two scripts and explain why they do the same thing.

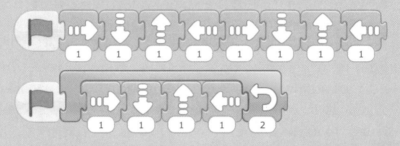

TIPS FOR GROWN-UPS

When you wrap a series of blocks in a Repeat block, you will see a gray shadow from the Repeat block appear in the programming area before you drop it. This shadow will show you exactly which blocks will fall inside the Repeat block.

You can still add blocks in after you've dropped the Repeat block, so don't worry if you can't get the shadow to wrap around all the blocks you want.

PROJECT TiME! OLD MACDONALD'S FARM

For this project you will make a farm with three animals and a barn, and you will program the animals to start moving when you tap the Green Flag button. You will use the skills that you learned in this chapter: move, turn, show, hide, and repeat.

HOW TO MAKE IT

Let's make a farm with at least three animals.

1. To set the scene, we can find a background that will give the animals a good place to graze. Tap the **Change Background** button, tap the farm, and then tap the check mark to load the farm onto the stage.

2. Now we can add the farm animals. Let's start with a rabbit. Tap the plus sign under the cat to add a new character. Select the rabbit and then tap the check mark.

3. We want to make the rabbit disappear, reappear, and then move in different directions when we tap the Green Flag button. Drag the following blocks to the programming area, and snap them together to make this script:

4. Now that you've created a script for the rabbit, can you add more animals to your scene and create programs for them so that they also move when you tap the Green Flag button?

Add at least two more animals to your farm, and give them programs to make the animals move around the stage. You might add a chicken that hops around using the Hop block. Or you can add a pig that turns around in circles. Perhaps you might add a cow and use the Move Left and Move Right blocks with a Repeat Forever block to keep it moving.

Which animals are going to be on your farm? Add different animals if you want to!

If you add a chicken and a pig, your farm will look like this:

5. You can see that this farm doesn't have a cat. To delete the cat from your project, press and hold it. When the red X appears, tap it to delete the cat. You can also delete the cat by pressing and holding it on the stage instead of in the list of characters.

6. You can also see that this farm has a barn. The barn is one of the characters that you can add to your project. Try adding it to your farm too.

HINTS

Note that when you have multiple characters in your project, and each character has a script that begins with the Start on Green Flag block, you should start the action by tapping the Green Flag button at the top of the screen. If, instead, you tap the Start on Green Flag block in your script, only the selected character will move.

LOOKING FOR A CHALLENGE?

Can you put yourself on the farm? Create a character that looks like you! Here's how you can do it. Tap the new character button, pick a person with a blank face, and tap the check mark.

To add your own face to the character, you'll have to edit it. Tap the **Paintbrush** button next to the character you chose.

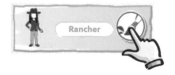

The paint editor opens. To add your face, tap the Camera tool, and then tap the face of the character.

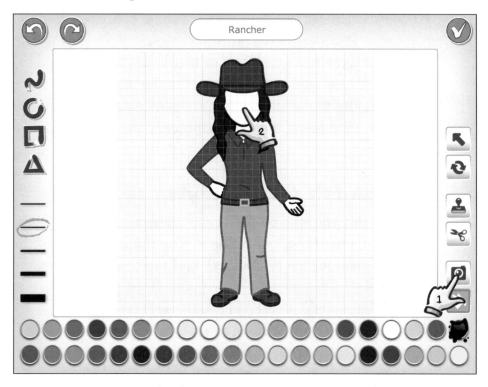

You'll now be able to take a photo.

Line up your own face so it looks good, and then tap the **Camera** button. You're really in ScratchJr now!

MAKING CONNECTIONS

LITERACY CONNECTION:
BUILDING NEW VOCABULARY

Go over the vocabulary for the different kinds of animals that live on a farm. Can you use any of these new words in your Old MacDonald project?

Remember, you can add text to your project, create characters that look like letters, or even rename existing characters!

MATH CONNECTION:
COUNTING THE BLOCKS YOU'VE USED

Count the number of blocks in your project. How many blue (motion), yellow (triggering), and purple (looks) blocks did you use? Create a chart or graph showing the different blocks you used. Which block color did you use the most?

TIPS FOR GROWN-UPS

If some characters do not move when you tap the Green Flag button at the top of the screen, double-check that the scripts for all of the characters begin with a Start on Green Flag block.

Sometimes children may get frustrated because their character is not moving in the way that they expected. Explain that an important part of the programming process is *debugging*—that is, testing your program, figuring out what went wrong, and then improving the program.

CHAPTER 3
STORIES

You can make your own stories with ScratchJr by adding dialogue and new scenes to your animations. Invent new characters who talk to each other and travel to new places, just like in a story-book. With ScratchJr, you can make these stories come to life and play out before your eyes like a movie!

In the six activities in this chapter, you'll learn how to make your characters talk, how to move them through scenes, and how to control the speed and timing in your project.

Lastly, we'll create a "Tortoise and the Hare" story project that uses all of these features.

ACTIVITY 6: FIND YOUR VOICE!

Have the cat perform a show with words and sounds! You can record a song or sound for the cat to perform and write words in speech bubbles for the cat to say.

WHAT YOU'LL LEARN

In this activity, you will learn how to record sounds for your character and how to make speech bubbles that show your character talking.

play
Recorded
sound

say

HOW TO MAKE IT

1. Select the theatre background. Then, start the cat's script with a **Start on Green Flag** block.

2. Tap the green blocks category to show the *sound blocks* in the palette. Tap the **Microphone** button to go into the ScratchJr recording studio.

3. Here you can tap the **Record** button to record a sound, tap the **Stop** button to stop recording, and tap the **Play** button to play the sound you recorded.

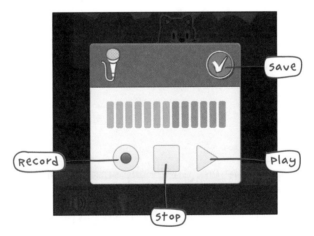

The green sound bars show you how loud the sounds are while you're recording them. More green bars mean a louder sound recording.

4. When you are happy with your sound, tap the check mark
    to save it. Your sound will be saved as a new Play Recorded
    Sound block that you can add to your script.

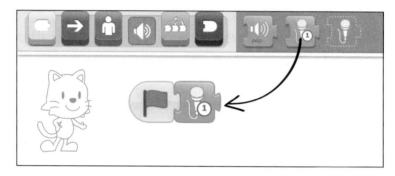

5. You can also have your characters talk with speech bubbles.
    Tap the purple blocks category to reveal the looks blocks in
    the palette. Drag the **Say** block to the programming area and
    snap it onto the end of your script.

6. Tap the white box under the speech bubble and delete the text
    there by tapping the backspace key. Now type what you want
    the cat to say and tap **Go**. If you type a longer speech for your
    character to say, the speech bubble will appear on the stage for
    longer so that you have time to read it all.

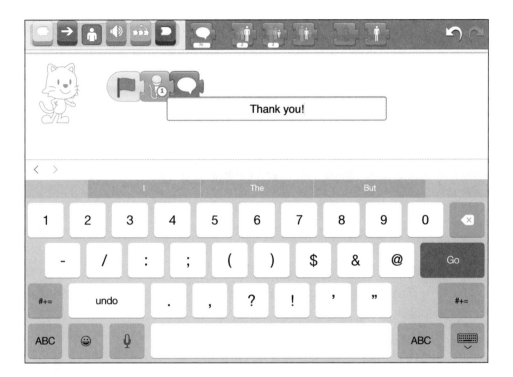

7. When you're ready, tap the **Green Flag** button at the top of the screen to see the show!

HINTS

Before you have saved your recording, you can play it back to hear it. If you don't like it, simply press the Record button again to record another sound.

Play Recorded Sound blocks appear in the green palette only after you have recorded a sound and saved it. You can keep up to five sounds for each character on each page of a project. (You'll learn how to add multiple pages in "Activity 7: Turn the Page!" on page 58.)

If you want to delete a sound, press and hold (*long-press*) the Play Recorded Sound block.

You will see a red X appear. Tap the X to delete the sound.

LOOKING FOR A CHALLENGE?

Can you make sounds and speech bubbles play at the same time? Make two scripts for the same character. Put both scripts in the character's programming area and begin both scripts with a **Start on Green Flag** block, but don't connect them together!

Hint: one script should have only Play Recorded Sound blocks.

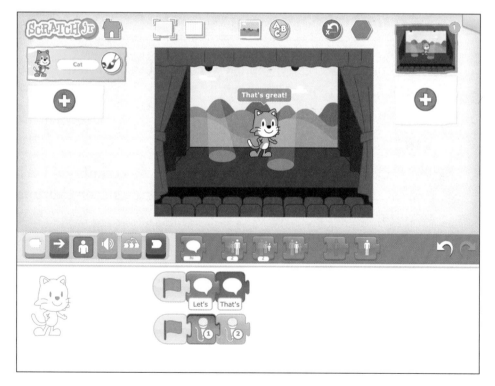

MAKING CONNECTIONS

LITERACY CONNECTION: PRESENTING

Use a combination of speaking, singing, and typing words to complete your performing cat's script. Practice speaking clearly when you record sounds so that other people can understand the story you have created.

You can always re-record your sounds until they are clear. Use the best sound recording you can make for your script. When you are finished, see if you can talk about your scripts with a friend or two and answer their questions.

MATH CONNECTION: ADDING AND SUBTRACTING

Now that your cat is singing in the performance, try making it dance too! Use the blue motion blocks to control your cat's dance moves. Count how many times you make your cat hop, move right, and move left in the dance. What is the total number of dance moves in your script? If you take away all of the Hop blocks, how many dance moves are there now?

TIPS FOR GROWN-UPS

Make sure that your device allows recording through a microphone and that the volume is turned up when you play the sound.

Troubleshooting iPads: when you first downloaded ScratchJr, it asked permission to use your microphone and camera. If you answered "no" to that question but want to use the microphone now, go to Settings on your device, find ScratchJr in your list of apps, and allow ScratchJr to access the microphone and camera.

Sounds cannot be copied to different characters. Each recorded sound is saved to a specific character (in a specific page and project) and can be used only in that character's scripts. Make sure children know which character's sounds they are creating.

ACTiViTY 7: TURN THE PAGE!

Let's make a story about your school! So far, all of the action in your story has happened in one place. In this activity, you will see how you can set different backgrounds for different scenes in your story, like turning pages in a book.

You can show a character traveling through your school by making a new page in ScratchJr for each part of your school that your character will visit.

WHAT YOU'LL LEARN

In this activity, you will learn how to create multiple pages in ScratchJr. After you create the new pages and add backgrounds and characters to them, you'll learn how to use the Go to Page block to tell your story from beginning to end without stopping.

Go To
Page

HOW TO MAKE IT

In this example, we will use three different rooms from a school: a classroom, a gym, and one more room that you can choose.

1. Start by selecting the classroom background, and pick a character to tell the story.

2. Cats are not allowed at school, so press and hold the cat character on the left, and then tap the red X to delete the cat.

3. Give your character something to do in this scene. For now, we will just have her move across the classroom when we tap the **Green Flag** button.

4. When you are ready to add a new page, tap the plus sign on the right side of the screen.

Now you have a whole new space to add the next part of your story!

It looks like you have started a whole new project, but you can see that your classroom scene is in the list of pages on the right side of the screen. You have only turned the page.

5. Pick a background for page 2. This time, let's choose the gym.

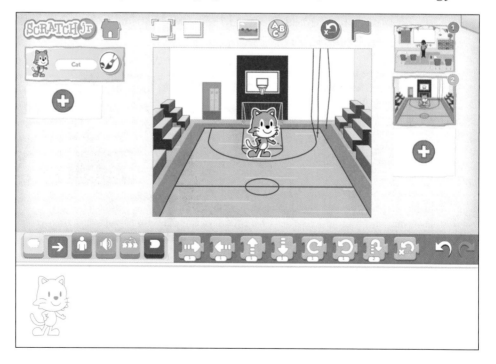

6. We want the same character from page 1 to be on this page, so add the girl as you did before and delete the cat.

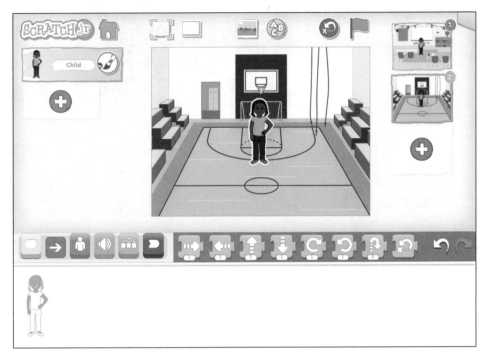

7. In the gym, let's have the girl say "Time to exercise!" and jump up and down a few times.

8. Now add a third page with a background that looks like another room in your school. We've chosen the library. Add the girl, delete the cat, and decide on an action that your character should take.

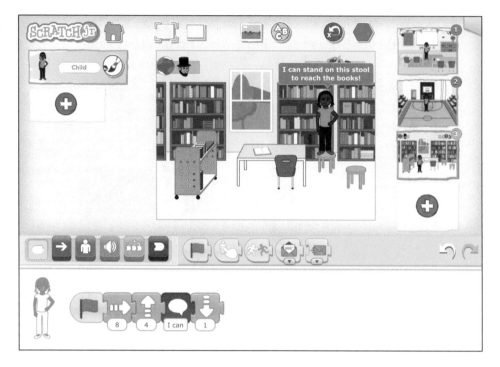

In our example, the girl walks over to a stool, climbs onto it, and says "I can stand on this stool to reach the books!"

9. When all of your pages are complete, it is time to connect them so that the action flows from one page to the next. Tap the first page in the list to go back to it.

10. Now tap the red blocks category to reveal the *end blocks*. Each new page you create makes a new Go to Page block with a small picture of your new page (called a *thumbnail*) in it.

End Blocks

You have a Go to Page block for every page in your project.

11. Use the **Go to Page 2** block at the end of your character's script on the first page.

When this script finishes, it will "turn the page" and go to the second page of your story.

12. Now tap the second page, and add the **Go to Page 3** block to the end of the script there.

13. Tap the first page to return to it. Now when you tap the **Green Flag** button at the top of the screen, the action will flow through the pages without stopping. Every time a new page starts, all of its scripts that begin with a Start on Green Flag block will run automatically.

HINTS

As you add characters and pages, ScratchJr will keep track of them for you on the screen. The characters appear on the left, and the pages appear on the right. You can delete a character or a page from these lists by pressing and holding it and then tapping the red X that appears. You can change the order of the pages in the list by dragging them before or after other pages.

You can copy a character and its scripts from one page to another by dragging the character from the character area to the page thumbnail.

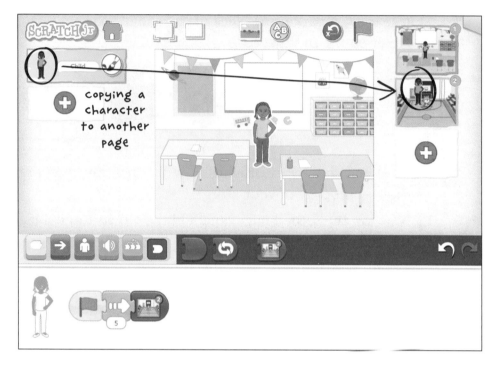

You can then change the script of the character on the new page, and it will not affect the script of that character on the original page.

LOOKING FOR A CHALLENGE?

Does your story have a title? Let's add one to the stage! Tap the **Add Text** button at the top and type the title of your tale.

You can change the size of your title by tapping the **Change Size** button, which looks like three A's. You can also change the color of your title by tapping the **Change Color** button, which looks like a paint bucket. Try it!

You can move the text around the page by dragging it, just like you can with a character. You could even write something on the whiteboard in the classroom!

MAKING CONNECTIONS

LITERACY CONNECTION:
TELLING YOUR OWN STORIES

Use ScratchJr to tell a story that actually happened to you! Use multiple pages to make sure your story has a beginning, middle, and end. Try including more pictures and words to tell your story. Don't forget to share it with a friend when you're all done!

MATH CONNECTION: SEQUENCING YOUR STORY

Make new pages and put them in order. Practice counting forward each time your story moves to the next page. How many pages does your story have? Are your pages in the correct order?

TIPS FOR GROWN-UPS

If the action does not automatically continue after the script has turned to a new page, make sure your scripts have a Start on Green Flag block.

To show your entire story from the start, make sure the first page is currently selected when you tap the **Green Flag** button. If you are on a different page when you tap the Green Flag button, the action will start on that page and continue to the end, without going through the first part of your story.

ACTIVITY 8: CHANGE THE PACE!

Make two characters race each other! Who will win? You decide!

WHAT YOU'LL LEARN

In this activity, you will learn how to use the Set Speed block to tell each character how fast to move.

set speed

HOW TO MAKE IT

1. For this race, we'll choose the savannah background.

2. Delete the cat, and add the zebra and the monkey.

3. Let's make a script for the zebra first. Begin your script with a **Start on Green Flag** block.

4. Now, tap the orange blocks category to show the control blocks. You can use the **Set Speed** block to make characters go slowly or quickly.

When you tap the arrow at the bottom of the Set Speed block, it gives you three options: Slow, Medium, and Fast.

This changes the speed of any action block you put in the script after the Set Speed block.

Your characters will all move at medium speed unless you use the Set Speed block to make them go slower or quicker.

5. In this activity, we want the zebra to go slower . . .

. . . and the monkey to go faster.

6. Tap the **Green Flag** button at the top and watch them race! Can you change the race to have a different winner? Can you make it a tie?

HINTS

Since the scripts for the zebra and the monkey are so similar, we can take a shortcut. After making the zebra's script, copy it to the monkey by dragging it from the zebra's programming area over to the monkey in the character area on the left side of the stage.

Now choose the monkey and just change the speed in the **Set Speed** block in the script that you copied.

copying a script to another character

LOOKING FOR A CHALLENGE?

Now that you have used the Set Speed block to make your characters race, try to see how else you can use it. Can you make a character shrink slowly or grow quickly? Can you make a character disappear in the blink of an eye or fade away slowly?

You can use more than one Set Speed block in one script. Can you make your character move slowly at first and then very fast? Or run really fast and then slow down? Try different combinations to see how your character can move.

Remember that the Set Speed block affects all the action blocks that come after it.

MAKING CONNECTIONS

LITERACY CONNECTION: CREATING ANNOUNCEMENTS

Use the **Add Text** button at the top of the stage to create an announcement that the race is beginning! After the race is over, add a second page to your story and type an announcement about who won (monkey or zebra) at the top of that page.

Hint: go back to "Activity 7: Turn the Page!" on page 58 if you need a reminder of how to move from page 1 to page 2.

MATH CONNECTION: TIMING THE RACE

Keep time! Count how many seconds it takes the monkey to complete the race and how many seconds it takes the zebra. Compare the numbers. Which number is larger? Which animal had the fastest time?

TIPS FOR GROWN-UPS

It can help to explain the different speeds as "Walk, Jog, and Run" instead of "Slow, Medium, and Fast."

When you drag a script to another character to copy it over, you should see the script return to the programming area of the first character. If the script disappears entirely, then it's possible that you did not actually reach the target character before letting go of the script that you were dragging. In that case, ScratchJr will think that you are deleting the script. If this happens, just tap the **Undo** button on the blocks palette, and the script should reappear.

Note that when you set the speed of a character in a script, the character will keep moving at that speed until you set a new speed. For example, the first time you run the following script, the character will move down at normal speed and then move up quickly. But when you run the script a second time, the character will move down quickly and up quickly because it is still set to Fast.

To avoid this, you can set speeds at the beginning or end of the script to reset the character to its initial speed.

ACTIVITY 9: STOP AND LOOK!

Help the cat cross the street safely by pausing first at the sidewalk!

WHAT YOU'LL LEARN

In this activity, you will use a Wait block to make the action pause for a few seconds.

wait

HOW TO MAKE IT

1. Select the suburbs background and position your cat at the top of the grass next to the house.

2. Start your script with a **Start on Green Flag** block, and then use the **Move Down** block to have the cat take two steps toward the sidewalk.

  Make sure the cat isn't already in the road! If two steps are too many, have the cat take one step instead.

3. Now, tap the orange blocks category to show the control blocks, and then drag the **Wait** block to your script.

4. You can tap the number input at the bottom of the Wait block to change the amount of time you want the cat to wait. The number is given in tenths of a second. Let's change the number to **20** so that the cat will wait 2 seconds before crossing the street.

5. After waiting at the side of the street, the cat can safely cross, so have it move down another four steps to reach the other side of the street.

6. When you run the script by tapping the **Green Flag** button at the top of the screen, the script will pause when it reaches the Wait block, and then it will continue with the last block. This makes the cat move from the grass to the edge of the road, pause, and then cross the street.

LOOKING FOR A CHALLENGE?

Try to program a car that crosses the road in front of the cat.
Time the car so that it goes along the road while the cat is waiting. Can you make the cat wait long enough so that it crosses
safely after the car has passed?

MAKING CONNECTIONS

LITERACY CONNECTION: ADDING NARRATION

What does your cat want to say during different parts of the story? Use the **Say** block to add narration. Can't think of what to make the cat say? Have it tell a silly story or a funny joke!

MATH CONNECTION: CHANGING THE WAIT TIME

Practice changing the numbers on the Wait block to make your cat wait for different amounts of time. What number should you enter to make your cat wait 2 seconds? How about 4 seconds?

TIPS FOR GROWN-UPS

The number on the Wait block is measured in tenths of a second. So if the Wait block has a 50 on it, the character will wait 5 seconds. You can help your child understand this by counting seconds out loud.

ACTIVITY 10: WAIT YOUR TURN!

You can use the Wait block to control how two characters interact with each other. In this activity, the horse agrees to give the cat a ride and they gallop off together!

WHAT YOU'LL LEARN

The Wait block can pause the action for a character long enough to let another character say or do something.

HOW TO MAKE IT

1. First, choose the farm background, and then add the horse. You can leave the cat where it is, but you need to move the horse to the left edge of the stage, as in the pictures shown here. We want to arrange the cat and the horse so that they move together.

2. Let's make a script for the cat first. Use a **Say** block to have the cat say, "May I have a ride?"

3. Add a **Wait** block to have the cat wait for 2 seconds (**20** tenths of a second) while the horse answers and walks over to it.

4. Then move the cat forward 6 steps with the horse.

5. Now tap the horse to make its script. First, add a **Wait** block set to 2 seconds (**20** tenths of a second) to give the cat time to ask for a ride. Then, add a **Say** block to have the horse reply, "Sure!" Then move the horse forward 11 steps.

6. Now when you tap the **Green Flag** button at the top, the cat and the horse will speak, and then the horse will give the cat a ride to the end of the field!

HINTS

Try to build your scripts so that the cat and the horse move together at the same time. It may take a few tries to get the cat and horse positioned just right so that it looks like the cat is riding on the horse's back when they move forward.

LOOKING FOR A CHALLENGE?

After the horse says "Sure!" see if you can have the cat answer "Thanks!" You will have to add another **Wait** block for the horse so that it waits for the cat to respond before moving forward. Try to figure out how much time you need to add for this.

Can you also time it so that the cat gets off the horse and says "Thanks!" again when the ride is over?

MAKING CONNECTIONS

LITERACY CONNECTION: USING FULL SENTENCES

Make sure you use full sentences when making the characters speak to each other.

MATH CONNECTION: COUNTING THE WAIT TIME

If you want to increase the time on a Wait block, count how much time you need and replace the number on the block with your new time.

TIPS FOR GROWN-UPS

Coordinating a conversation between two characters is tricky. It requires a lot of trial and error, and if you make any changes to the action or to the dialogue, you will need to adjust the numbers on your Wait blocks. To coordinate actions and speech more precisely and systematically, you can use the Start on Message and Send Message blocks. You will learn about these blocks in Chapter 4.

One tip for making it look like the cat is sitting on the horse is to add the horse to the project last or to move it slightly. The last character you move or add in ScratchJr will be "on top" (in the foreground), and when the horse is on top, the animation will look a little nicer.

ACTiVITY 11: BUILD A SNOWMAN!

ScratchJr includes a powerful paint editor that you can use to draw and change characters and backgrounds. For example, you can build your own snowman to live in the arctic!

WHAT YOU'LL LEARN

In this activity, you will learn how to use the paint editor to make your own characters! You can also change other characters and backgrounds using the paint editor. Whenever you see the paint editor button, it means you can edit that object or create your own object.

HOW TO MAKE IT

1. Start your project by choosing the arctic background.

2. To draw a character, tap the plus sign on the left side of the screen as if you were going to add a new character.

3. Without actually selecting a character, tap the **Paintbrush** button to open the paint editor.

4. Now, to make a snowman, you will need three circles of different sizes. To make a circle, tap the **Circle** tool.

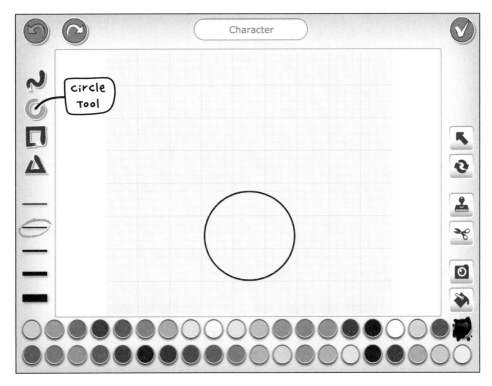

5. Next, drag your finger on the drawing grid (or *canvas*) in a diagonal line, and you will see a circle appear. When you get the size and shape that you want for the snowman's base, lift your finger off the grid. Make another circle for the snowman's middle. Don't worry about where it is on the grid, because you can move it.

6. Tap the **Drag** tool, and then drag the circle where you want it.

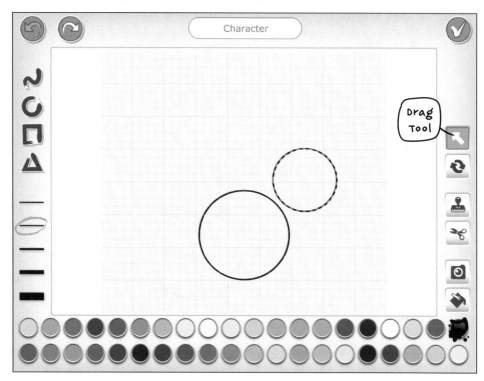

If you tap on the drawing instead of dragging it, little circles will appear on the lines that let you change the shape. We want our snowman to have round snowballs, so be careful not to drag one of these little circles, or you might accidentally change the round shape.

7. Make a third circle for the snowman's head and drag it into place too.

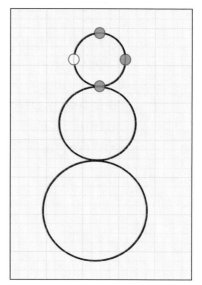

8. Now you need to make the eyes with two much smaller circles. Using the Circle tool, draw a small circle, or just tap the screen to create a round dot. You can make sure your eye circles are the same size by using the Duplicate tool, which makes a copy of the shape you choose. Tap the **Duplicate** tool (which looks like a stamp), and then tap the eye circle that you want to copy.

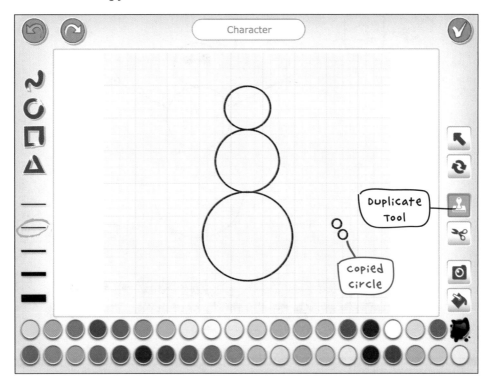

The Duplicate tool makes a copy of the shape that appears just to the side of the original, so you need to drag them apart carefully. Drag these eyes into place on the snowman's head.

9. Tap the **Line** tool and draw two arms for the snowman. Next, we need to fill in the snowballs with white paint. Tap the **Fill** tool (which looks like a paint bucket) and select white from the color palette. Then tap each snowball, and the shape will fill with the color that you chose. Select black and color the eyes.

10. To make a carrot for the nose, change the color to orange and tap the **Triangle** tool. Drag your finger diagonally anywhere on the canvas until you have a carrot-shaped triangle. Then, using the **Fill** tool, paint the carrot orange.

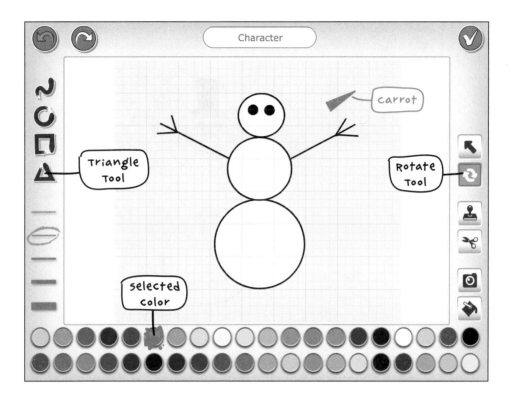

11. The Rotate tool turns items around, and you can use it to arrange the carrot like a nose. To do so, tap the **Rotate** tool, and then press and hold the carrot. Keep your finger on the screen and move it up or down or side to side to turn the carrot. Use the **Drag** tool to drag the carrot into place on the snowman's face.

Ta-da! You've created your own unique character! Don't forget that you can give your snowman a name with the text bar at the top. You can also add more features to your snowman, such as a hat, a smile, or some buttons. Tap the check mark at the top right when you are satisfied with your snowman, and it will appear in your arctic scene.

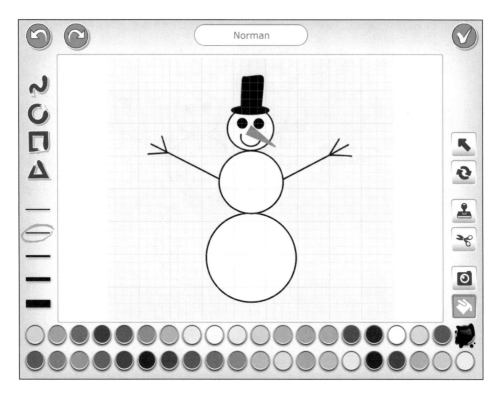

Now you can give your snowman and the cat a script to tell your winter story!

HINTS

If you tap a character before tapping the Paintbrush button, the paint editor will open with that character on the canvas instead of with a blank canvas. This allows you to edit existing characters with the paint editor. Your modified character is saved as a new character—it won't replace the original character. So go ahead and make a blue cat or a pig with polka dots! Any new or modified characters that you make will be saved in your character menu so you can use them in all of your projects.

If you make a mistake with your character, you can use the Undo button at the top. If you want to delete something in particular, you can use the Cut tool (which looks like a pair of scissors).

Just tap the Cut tool, and then tap what you want to delete. Make sure you tap a different button afterward to continue painting, or you'll end up cutting everything out!

LOOKING FOR A CHALLENGE?

See if you can figure out how to edit the arctic background.

Write a script to show the cat building a snowman by making a new page for each step of the snowman building. So on page 1 have the cat build the bottom snowball, on page 2 have the cat add the middle snowball, and on page 3 have the cat put on the snowman's head and arms.

MAKING CONNECTIONS

LITERACY CONNECTION: ASKING QUESTIONS

As you are using the paint editor, you may need extra help
finding the tool that you want. Don't be afraid to ask your
classmates or an adult!

MATH CONNECTION: COUNTING THE CIRCLES

Count the circles as you add them to the snowman to make sure
that the three circles of the body plus the two circles of the eyes
make five circles.

TIPS FOR GROWN-UPS

When filling in the circles of the snowman with white paint, children might find it difficult to tell the difference between a filled
circle and an unfilled one. Try selecting a more visible color just
to show them how the Fill tool works. Then go back to white and
fill the circles for the snowman.

Appendix B has a quick reference guide for all the tools in
the paint editor.

PROJECT TiME! THE TORTOISE AND THE HARE

Now you can use all of the skills you've just learned to make a full story! This story is about a race between a patient tortoise and a boastful hare. To create the scene, you first have to make a tortoise with the paint editor. Then, you can use the Set Speed block to make the hare move faster than the tortoise and to help the tortoise win! You will also use what you learned about making characters talk to each other and about turning story pages.

HOW TO MAKE IT

1. Choose the farm background, delete the cat, and add the rabbit character.

2. We don't have a tortoise character already made, so we'll use the paint editor to make one. Make sure you paint the tortoise quite big! It will look smaller when it appears in the scene than it does in the paint editor.

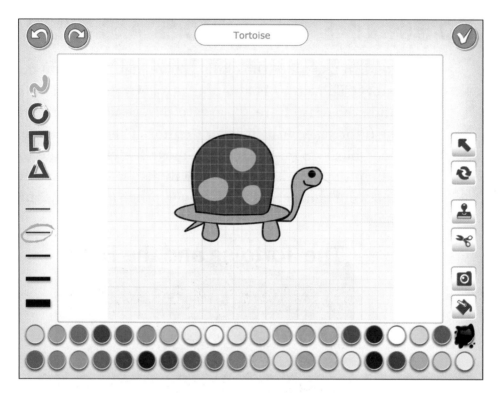

3. The race will go over the farm, past a river, and through an orchard. For this we need to make two new pages. Add the river background to the second page and then add the spring background to the third page.

4. Let's add the tortoise and the hare to the two new pages too. Drag the rabbit character from page 1 to page 2 to copy it over, and then drag the tortoise from page 1 to page 2. Don't forget to copy the characters to page 3 too.

5. You can use the Add Text button to add words of different sizes and colors to your page. Larger words look more like a title, and smaller words might be the main part of your story that you can read aloud. Select page 1 and tap the **Add Text** button to give your story a title.

6. Now comes the action. On page 1, the tortoise and the hare talk about the race they want to have.

7. We'll start you off with the script to begin the race. Then, can you write the scripts to show what happens next in your story?

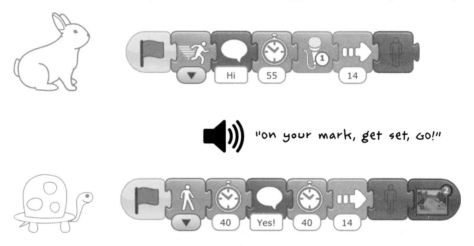

"on your mark, get set, GO!"

Here are some tricks you may need:

- You don't want your hare to look like it's waiting if it gets to the end of the page first! You can use the **Set Speed** block (set to **Fast**) and the **Hide** block to make the hare run to the end of the page and disappear. Use this trick to keep characters off the page when you don't need them! Make sure to reset the speed of your character if you want it to slow down once it reappears.

- You can record sounds to add excitement to your story!

- Fables like "The Tortoise and the Hare" usually have a *moral* at the end—a sentence explaining what the characters learned. You can use the **Add Text** button to display a moral at the end of your story. Use the **Change Size** button to adjust the size of the words to fit your page.

HINTS

Remember, the Set Speed block does not slow down or speed up the timing of Wait blocks.

When you have more than one character, you need to add the Go to Page block to the script of only one of the characters to turn the page. But be careful about which script ends with the Go to Page block. Some scripts will finish sooner than others, and the page may turn before all the characters have finished their scripts. You want to add the Go to Page block to the script that takes the longest to finish.

LOOKING FOR A CHALLENGE?

Try recording yourself telling the story by using multiple **Play Recorded Sound** blocks. Can you time the recorded sounds with the actions on the screen?

MAKING CONNECTIONS

LITERACY CONNECTION: CREATING A DIGITAL BOOK

When programming this story, you'll use a combination of drawing, writing, and speaking to create an animated tale about the tortoise and the hare! Practice writing and spelling by using the **Say** block to make speech bubbles for the characters and the **Add Text** button to add titles. When your story is finished, read your digital storybook to a friend! Practice speaking clearly and loudly to describe what is happening as your scripts are running.

MATH CONNECTION: MAKING CHARACTERS MOVE

Use numbers, counting, and guesswork to control the way the characters move with the blue motion blocks. You will need to experiment with different numbers in the motion blocks to make your characters move the way you want. Can you make the same action happen using fewer blocks just by changing the numbers? If you want your characters to move to exact spots on the stage, try tapping the **Grid** button (at the top of the screen), and use the numbers on the grid as your guide!

TIPS FOR GROWN-UPS

It will likely take children many tries to create a complete narrative with multiple pages and dialogue. Allow them to focus on one aspect of the story at a time, and encourage testing and retesting of scripts along the way. This lets them quickly find and repair *bugs*, or things that happen differently than expected, in their scripts.

It is frustrating for anyone to lose unsaved work! Remember to save your work often by tapping the **Home** button at the top of the screen. When you see the project in your project library, it is saved. Tap the project's image again to reopen it and continue working.

CHAPTER 4
GAMES

You've already made some animations and stories. But in this chapter you'll learn how to make games! You'll make four different small games, and then you'll use everything you've learned to make one big game at the end.

ACTiViTY 12: PiCK A PEACH!

The goal of this game is to find out which of the peaches on the tree is ripe! Tap a peach, and if it's ready, it'll fall to the ground.

To create this game, we'll need to give scripts to a peach on the tree.

WHAT YOU'LL LEARN

Until now, you could start all of your scripts by tapping the Green Flag button. In this activity, you will learn how to start a script by tapping a character, using the Start on Tap block. You will also see how to use the Shrink block, the Go Home block, and the Reset Characters button.

start   shrink   Go Home   Reset
on Tap   characters

HOW TO MAKE IT

1. Select the summer background and delete the cat character. You can see that the tree on the left already has some peaches on it, but these are just part of the background and they cannot move. To get a peach that will move when we tap it, we need to add it to our scene as a character.

2. To do this, tap the plus sign in the character area and select the peach. Drag the peach onto the tree that already has three peaches on it.

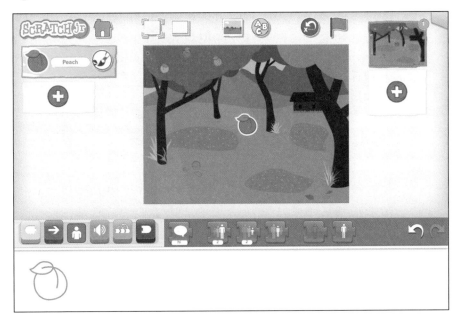

3. We want to make the peach close to the same size as the other peaches on the tree, so tap the purple looks blocks category. Drag the **Shrink** block to your peach's programming area and tap it twice. The first tap will make the peach smaller, and the second tap will make it even smaller.

4. Now the peach is the right size, so you can drag the **Shrink** block back to the blocks palette to delete it.

5. Tap the yellow triggering blocks category to show the family of starting blocks. This time, instead of using the Start on Green Flag block, we're going to use the Start on Tap block, which brings characters to life when you tap them.

6. Drag the **Start on Tap** block to the programming area to start the peach's script. Add some blue motion blocks to this triggering block to make the peach wiggle and fall from the tree.

7. Try it out! Tap the peach and see what happens.

We need to do one more thing to make this game easier to play over and over. If you tap the peach again after it has fallen to the ground, the peach will start its script again but from the ground, not from the tree. The Start on Tap block does not return characters to their original positions like the Start on Green Flag block does.

You can return the peach to the tree by tapping the **Reset Characters** button at the top of the screen.

The Reset Characters button will return all characters to their home positions.

If you have other characters moving around on the stage and you want only the peach to return home, then you might prefer to reset just the peach.

8. Tap the blue motion blocks category to find the Go Home block.

9. Drag the **Go Home** block to the end of the peach's script.

Now the peach will hop back up onto the tree after it has fallen, and you can play the game again!

HINTS

You might want the script to pause for a couple of seconds before it reaches the Go Home block so that the peach doesn't jump straight back up onto the tree as soon as it falls. Use the **Wait** block to make the peach stay on the ground for a moment.

LOOKING FOR A CHALLENGE?

To make the game more interesting, you could add more peaches to the tree. Can you make it so that some of the fruit is not ripe enough to fall yet? If the fruit is not ripe, maybe it just wiggles on the tree and stays put.

MAKING CONNECTIONS

LITERACY CONNECTION: ADDING TO THE STORY

Add another character to this scene and create the first page of a story! How do the characters react to the falling fruit? Are they surprised? Hungry? Use speech bubbles, sound recordings, and the **Add Text** button to incorporate speaking and words into your story. You can look back at Chapters 2 and 3 if you need help remembering how to do this. Swap projects with a friend and complete each other's stories by adding a new page!

MATH CONNECTION:
COMPOSING AND COMPARING SHAPES

Now that you have made a falling peach, try creating different types of fruits. What shapes do you use? Which fruits are the biggest? Use descriptive words to compare and contrast the various shapes and sizes you used.

TIPS FOR GROWN-UPS

It is sometimes difficult for young children to tap a character lightly and evenly enough for ScratchJr to interpret the motion as a tap and not a drag. If ScratchJr thinks the motion is a drag, it will move the peach slightly instead of running the script. If the peach does not wiggle and fall from the tree when the child taps it, that's the likely cause.

ACTIVITY 13: BLAST OFF!

In this activity, the cat counts down, and then a rocket ship blasts off!

WHAT YOU'LL LEARN

You'll learn how to get the characters to work together, using the Send Message and Start on Message blocks. The cat will count down the seconds, and then the rocket will blast off!

send
message

start on
message

HOW TO MAKE IT

1. Start by adding the moon background and the rocket character.

2. Let's write the script for the cat first. Tap the cat to return to it. Drag a **Start on Green Flag** block to the programming area.

3. Tap the purple looks blocks category and add three **Say** blocks to make the cat count "3, 2, 1."

4. Tap the yellow triggering blocks category to find the Send Message block.

5. Drag the **Send Message** block down to the programming area and snap it onto the end of the cat's script.

This will tell the rocket when to start. When the cat has finished counting, it will send a message for the rocket to receive.

6. Now, let's tap the rocket and give it a script. We want to make the rocket ship blast off when it receives the message from the cat. Start the script with the **Start on Message** block. This script will run when another script sends a message.

7. After the Start on Message block, add a **Move Up** block to
    make the rocket move up the screen as if it is taking off, and
    then add a **Hide** block to make the rocket disappear.

8. Now, tap the **Green Flag** button to try out the script.

HINTS

This script uses an orange message. You can choose from six different message colors to communicate between characters in your
project. Just keep in mind that your Send Message block has to
match the color of your Start on Message block. For example, an
orange Send Message block will trigger a script that begins with
an orange Start on Message block, but if you have used a purple
Send Message block in your project instead, the script that begins
with an orange Start on Message block will never run!

LOOKING FOR A CHALLENGE?

Add some more characters and start each of their scripts with a **Start on Message** block. You could have a crowd of characters cheer together when the rocket blasts off by giving them all the same color Start on Message block.

Maybe you could have a shooting star fly across the sky as the rocket is rising. Would it start with the same color message as the crowd?

Remember that all scripts that begin with a Start on Message block of the same color will start at the same time when a Send Message block of that color is used.

MAKING CONNECTIONS

LITERACY CONNECTION:
GETTING READY FOR TAKEOFF

Before the countdown begins, program the cat to make an announcement about what is going to happen. Use the **Say** block and the **Add Text** button to prepare for the rocket's take-off. Where is the rocket going? When will it take off?

Add another page after the blastoff to show where the rocket travels!

MATH CONNECTION: COUNTING BACKWARD

Practice counting backward! Your cat is counting down the amount of time until the rocket ship will take off into space. When your cat reaches "1," the rocket ship will blast off. After programming the cat to count down from 3, try making it count down from 10, 15, and even 20!

TIPS FOR GROWN-UPS

You can explain the Send Message block as an announcement that one character makes to all of the other characters. Only the characters with a Start on Message block of the same color as the announcement will listen for the announcement and react to it. The rest of the characters will ignore it.

ACTiViTY 14: PLAY TAG!

Program the cat and the dog to play tag. In this game, the dog's script will start when it is tagged by the cat. Then the dog will tag the cat, and they'll continue to play tag until you stop the program.

WHAT YOU'LL LEARN

In this activity you'll learn how to use another new starting block: the Start on Bump block.

start on
Bump

The Start on Bump block starts a character's script when the character bumps into another character.

HOW TO MAKE IT

1. Select the farm background and add the dog. Position the cat and the dog on the stage so that they are standing about five steps apart. You can move them later on if those positions aren't quite right when you try out your script.

The cat will move toward the dog and say "Tag!" Then it will move back and pause for 2 seconds to wait for the dog to tag it. We'll add a **Repeat Forever** block to the cat's script so the cat and the dog will play again and again.

2. Create the following script for the cat:

3. The dog's script uses the **Start on Bump** block so that it starts when the dog is bumped by the cat.

After the dog is bumped, it will wait 2 seconds to give the cat a chance to run away. Then the dog will move to the cat, say "Tag!" and run away.

4. Create the following script for the dog:

We don't need the Repeat Forever block for the dog, because the Start on Bump block will run every time the dog is tagged.

5. Tap the **Green Flag** button to watch your characters play tag! Press the **Stop** button when you want the game to end.

HINTS

If a character is touching another character that has a Start on Bump script, the script will keep running until the characters are not touching anymore. For example, if you move the cat so close to the dog that they are touching, the dog's Start on Bump script will begin running, and it will continue to run over and over again until you move the cat away from the dog.

LOOKING FOR A CHALLENGE?

See if you can make a game of dodgeball. Add a ball to your project and make it move all around the stage with a few different **Start on Green Flag** scripts that repeat forever. (See "Looking for a Challenge?" on page 56 to see how to use two scripts together in the same programming area.) Change the scripts of the cat and the dog so that when they are hit by the ball, they say "I'm out!" and then disappear. Add more characters to make the game more exciting!

Remember that you can get your characters to talk and perform actions at the same time by using two scripts in the same programming area. Decide which scripts should start with a Start on Bump block and which ones should start with a Start on Green Flag block.

MAKING CONNECTIONS

LITERACY CONNECTION: CREATING A CONVERSATION BETWEEN FRIENDS

Use the **Say** block to get your cat and dog to talk to each other while they play. Use phrases like "I'm going to tag you!" and "You're it!" in the conversation, using capital letters and punctuation marks when needed. How does the game of tag end? Does someone give up? Remember to use the **Start on Bump** and **Wait** blocks to help time the conversation so it makes sense with the way the characters are moving.

MATH CONNECTION: ESTIMATING

To program the perfect game of tag, you will need to estimate what numbers to use on the Wait blocks and how many blue motion blocks you need. Try different numbers and test them out to see what works best with your program!

TIPS FOR GROWN-UPS

This activity repeats using a combination of the **Repeat Forever** block and the **Start on Bump** block. While it might seem like a good idea to give the cat a script that has a Start on Bump block just like the dog, this approach won't work!

If both characters have a Start on Bump block, they'll both be triggered at the same time. It doesn't matter which one is moving or which one is stationary when they "bump" into each other. The block will be triggered, and they won't bump again.

ACTIVITY 15: GUESS THE ODD ONE OUT!

Create a two-player guessing game to play with your friends and family. In this game, all of the animals are moving in a pattern, but one of them is moving slightly differently than the others. Each player takes turns guessing which animal is the odd one out. If the player chooses the wrong one, the animal will say, "Not I!" If the player guesses right, the animal will say, "You got it!" The first player to tap the correct animal wins.

WHAT YOU'LL LEARN

You'll learn three new things in this activity: how to use the Stop block, how to run a project in Presentation Mode, and how to use different triggering blocks to start different actions for the same character.

Stop

Enter Presentation Mode

Exit Presentation Mode

HOW TO MAKE IT

1. Pick a background. Your animals will need lots of space, so the farm background would be one good choice.

2. Add four animals to join the cat on the stage. You'll program four of the five animals to move in the same way and one of them to move differently.

3. Make a script for one animal to have it move around in a square. Add another script that makes it say "Not I!" when it is tapped.

4. Make the same scripts for three other animals so that four of the animals have the exact same scripts.

Note that instead of making a new script for each of the animals, you can copy a script from one animal to another by simply dragging the script from the programming area to the animal in the list of characters.

5. Change the time on each script's **Wait** block so that the animals will start moving at different times.

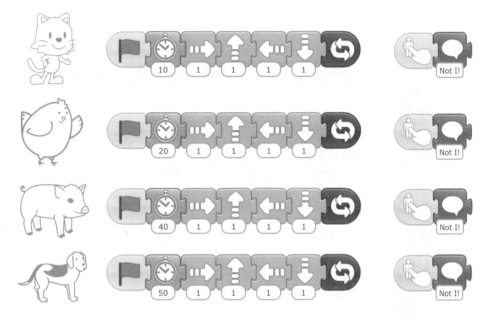

6. Add a script for the odd-one-out animal with an extra **Move Down** block to make the animal move slightly differently than the others. Then give it another script so that it stops and says "You're right!" when it is tapped. To make the animal stop moving when it's tapped, tap the orange control blocks category and drag a **Stop** block to the end of the animal's script.

7. When you're finished programming the animals, tap the **Enter Presentation Mode** button to hide the programming area so that no one accidentally sees the answer in the script.

The stage will fill the entire screen.

8. Now you have a game! Tap the **Green Flag** button to get it started, and see who can find the odd one out first.

9. Tap the **Exit Presentation Mode** button to return to the regular ScratchJr screen.

LOOKING FOR A CHALLENGE?

When the winning animal is tapped, it stops moving. See if you can make all of the other animals also stop moving when the game is won. You will have to use a **Send Message** block and give each of the other animals a **Start on Message** script that stops its motion.

MAKING CONNECTIONS

LITERACY CONNECTION:
WRITING THE GAME DIRECTIONS

How does the player know the rules of the game? Write step-by-step instructions for the player using **Say** blocks or the **Add Text** button. Can you give the players hints if they can't find the correct animal?

MATH CONNECTION:
WRITING YOUR OWN MATH PROBLEMS

The game you've created has a lot of different motion blocks and Wait blocks. Can you come up with a math problem worksheet for this game? You could write problems like "How many movements does the pig make?" or "Who is waiting the longest?"

Switch worksheets with a friend and answer each other's math problems! Don't forget to make an answer sheet and mark each other's answers.

TIPS FOR GROWN-UPS

The Stop block will stop the scripts for only the character that has the Stop block, not for any of the other characters. Once a script is stopped, you can restart it with the appropriate trigger (tapping the Green Flag, tapping the character, sending a message, and so on).

PROJECT TiME! CATS VERSUS BiRDS

Okay, you've learned a lot, so now let's make a really cool game. We'll make a one-player game where the bird must fly past three moving cats and touch the mushroom to win.

When the player taps the bird, it flies toward the mushroom, but if the bird touches any of the cats on the way, it has to go back to its starting position. If the bird reaches the mushroom safely, the player wins!

HOW TO MAKE IT

1. Choose a background for your game. The savannah is a good option because it has lots of sky for the bird to fly in.

2. Add a mushroom to your project and drag it to the right side of the stage. Then add a bird and drag it to the left side of the stage.

3. Now add two more cats and line them up in the middle of the stage so that they are not touching any of the other characters.

4. Program the cats to move upward at different speeds by changing the speed in the **Set Speed** block so it is different for each cat. You need to make another script to send an orange message when a cat is bumped by the bird so that the bird will know it has to go back to the start. Here is an example of our script for one cat:

5. Program the bird to move forward when it is tapped. Then add a script to make it go back to its home position when an orange message is sent because it bumped into a cat:

6. Program the mushroom to say "You win!" when it is bumped by the bird:

7. To play the game, tap the **Enter Presentation Mode** button.

You've just made a game that uses all the skills you learned in this chapter! When you play, your aim is to time the movement of the bird just right so that it dodges the moving cats and reaches the mushroom. Good luck!

HINTS

Make sure that the cats don't touch one another or the mushroom when they move around the screen. Bumps between any characters will send the bird back to the start, since the Start on Bump scripts are triggered by any bump, not just bumps from the bird.

LOOKING FOR A CHALLENGE?

Change the starting positions and speeds of the cats to make the game harder. What other strategies can you use to make this game easier or more difficult?

MAKING CONNECTIONS

LITERACY CONNECTION:
TURNING YOUR GAME INTO A STORY

Turn your game into a story! Make an introductory page explaining why the bird wants to reach the mushroom. Is there something special about this mushroom?

The second page can be the game, and the third page can be the ending to the story and a message to the player. For example, you might write something like "Congratulations, you reached the mushroom!"

MATH CONNECTION: KEEPING A TALLY

Get some friends to play this game with you. Keep a tally of the number of wins and losses for each person, and add them up once everyone has had the chance to play the same number of times. Did each player get a different result, or did every player have the same outcome?

TIPS FOR GROWN-UPS

When trying to tap the bird, a child may sometimes drag the bird instead. This will reset the home position of the bird to that new location, which may be in the middle of the screen. Then, when the bird bumps into a cat and returns to its home position, it will no longer go back to the edge of the stage.

To avoid this problem, add another character to the project— a star, for example—to act as a button; to make the bird move, you only have to tap this star. Place the star in the bottom corner of the stage where it will not touch any of the other characters.

The star should send a blue message when it is tapped, like this:

Change the bird's scripts so that it no longer moves forward when tapped. Instead, it moves forward when it receives the blue message from the star.

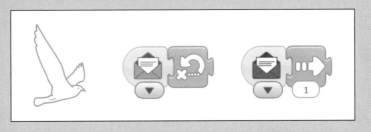

If the child drags the star while trying to tap it, that isn't a problem. The home position of the bird will stay the same, and the game can carry on.

AFTERWORD

Even though you've reached the end of the book, you are only just getting started with programming. The goal of this book is to guide you in helping the children in your life learn programming—

and, in the process, learn to design projects, solve problems, reason systematically, and express themselves creatively.

When your child has mastered all that ScratchJr has to offer, it might be time to introduce Scratch and its active online community. In Appendix A, you will find resources for this transition.

We have worked hard to bring coding to young children in a developmentally appropriate way. It is our strong belief that programming opens new ways of thinking and new forms of expression. We hope to continue making improvements to ScratchJr and creating new resources and opportunities for learning and sharing. We want ScratchJr to remain free so anyone, anywhere, can use it. So far, we have been able to do so through generous grants from the National Science Foundation and the Scratch Foundation. If you believe in our vision and want to support us, please consider making a donation to the Scratch Foundation (*http://www.scratchfoundation.org/*). Any amount, large or small, is appreciated.

Let's keep coding!

Marina and Mitch

APPENDIX A
TRANSITIONING FROM SCRATCHJR TO SCRATCH

When you're ready to take the next step in your programming journey, we recommend trying out Scratch, a programming tool designed for slightly older learners (ages 8 and up). Scratch offers additional features that enable children to create more advanced stories, games, and animations, but its basic programming approach is similar to ScratchJr, so it will feel familiar.

You will know that children are ready to move on to Scratch when they can tell a story or make a game independently with ScratchJr or when they are ready to start creating more advanced projects.

For example, children can use Scratch to do the following:

- Create games that keep score
- Import images and sounds
- Make characters move at any angle (not just up, down, left, and right)
- Program characters to change "costumes" within a project
- Create stories that are longer and more complex (more than four pages)

THE SCRATCH COMMUNITY

Perhaps the biggest difference between Scratch and ScratchJr is that Scratch is integrated into an online community, so it is easy for children to share their projects with one another, comment on one another's projects, and even remix one another's projects (that is, make variations of other people's projects using some of their characters and programming scripts).

This social dimension of Scratch is very appealing to many children and opens up opportunities for them to collaborate and learn from one another. But younger children might not be ready to participate in an online community. Before a child joins the Scratch community, you should make sure to have a discussion about appropriate online behavior. Also make sure to read the community guidelines on the Scratch website (*https:// scratch.mit.edu/community_guidelines/*).

GETTING STARTED WITH SCRATCH

Scratch runs in any web browser (such as Internet Explorer, Firefox, or Chrome) and on any type of laptop or desktop computer. To get started with Scratch, go to the Scratch website at *http://scratch.mit.edu/*. There you'll be able to explore more than 10 million projects created by other members of the Scratch community, and start creating your own projects. Click **Help** in the top navigation bar to see all the resources available to get you started and answer your questions.

If you want guided help with creating your first project, click the **Step-by-Step Intro**. You will see the project editor and a Tips sidebar with a step-by-step tutorial on how to make a project similar to the one that you made in Chapter 1 of this book.

If, instead, you want to get started on your own, you can click **Create** to go to the project editor and start programming. You can always view the Tips (on the right) to get help.

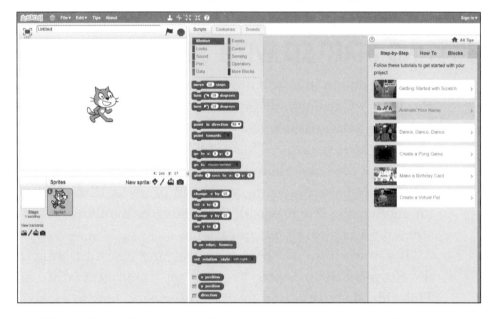

If you do not have a good Internet connection, or if you prefer not to participate in the Scratch online community, you can download an offline, stand-alone version of the Scratch programming editor from the Help page on the website.

THE SCRATCHED WEBSITE

ScratchEd (*http://scratched.gse.harvard.edu/*) is a separate online community specifically for educators who use Scratch. On the ScratchEd website, educators can share stories, exchange resources, and get support. Click the **Resources** tab to find the *Scratch Curriculum Guide*, a comprehensive guide with ideas, strategies, and activities for an introductory creative computing experience with Scratch.

The ScratchEd website and *Scratch Curriculum Guide* are developed by the ScratchEd Team at the Harvard Graduate School of Education.

APPENDIX B
REFERENCE GUIDES

This appendix provides additional information about the ScratchJr programming blocks and the paint editor. The "Block Reference" describes the ScratchJr blocks in all six categories. The "Paint Editor Reference" provides an explanation of all the features of the ScratchJr paint editor.

BLOCK REFERENCE

Here's a breakdown of all the blocks that are available in ScratchJr and what they do.

Triggering Blocks		
Block	**Name**	**Description**
	Start on Green Flag	Starts the script when the Green Flag is tapped.
	Start on Tap	Starts the script when you tap the character.
	Start on Bump	Starts the script when the character is touched by another character.
	Start on Message	Starts the script whenever a message of the specified color is sent.
	Send Message	Sends a message of the specified color.

Motion Blocks

Block	Name	Description
	Move Right	Moves the character a specified number of grid squares to the right.
	Move Left	Moves the character a specified number of grid squares to the left.
	Move Up	Moves the character a specified number of grid squares up.
	Move Down	Moves the character a specified number of grid squares down.
	Turn Right	Rotates the character clockwise a specified amount. Turn 12 for a full rotation.
	Turn Left	Rotates the character counter-clockwise a specified amount. Turn 12 for a full rotation.
	Hop	Moves the character up a specified number of grid squares and then down again.
	Go Home	Resets the character's location to its starting position. (To set a new starting position, drag the character to the location.)

Looks Blocks

Block	Name	Description
	Say	Shows a specified message in a speech bubble above the character.
	Grow	Increases the character's size.
	Shrink	Decreases the character's size.
	Reset Size	Returns the character to its default size.
	Hide	Fades out the character until it is invisible.
	Show	Fades in the character until it is visible.

Sound Blocks

Block	Name	Description
	Pop	Plays a "pop" sound.
	Play Recorded Sound	Plays a sound recorded by the user.

Control Blocks

Block	Name	Description
	Wait	Pauses the script for a specified amount of time (in tenths of seconds).
	Stop	Stops all of a character's scripts on the page.
	Set Speed	Changes the rate at which certain blocks are run.
	Repeat	Runs the blocks inside its loop a specified number of times.

End Blocks

Block	Name	Description
	End	Indicates the end of the script (but does not affect the script in any way).
	Repeat Forever	Runs the script over and over.
	Go to Page	Changes to the specified page of the project.

PAINT EDITOR REFERENCE

You can use the paint editor to draw your own characters and backgrounds or to customize existing ones.

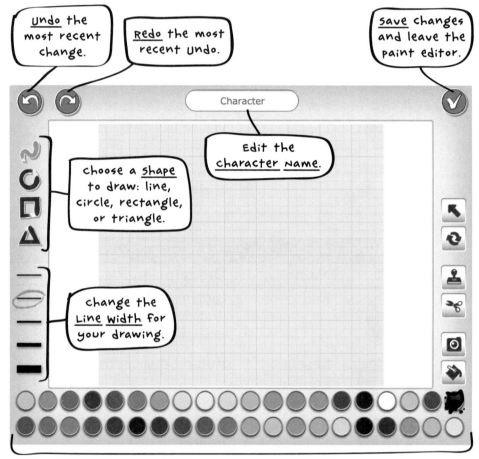

Undo the most recent change.

Redo the most recent undo.

save changes and leave the paint editor.

Character

Edit the character Name.

choose a shape to draw: line, circle, rectangle, or triangle.

change the Line width for your drawing.

select a color to use for drawing and filling in shapes.

Paint Editor Tools

Tool	Name	Description
	Drag	To move a character or shape on the canvas, select the Drag tool and drag the character or shape into place. When you tap a shape, small dots will appear, and you can drag these dots to alter the shape.
	Rotate	To turn a character or shape, select the Rotate tool, tap the character or shape, and drag your finger over the screen to rotate it around its center.
	Duplicate	To make a copy of something, select the Duplicate tool, and then tap the character or shape.
	Cut	To delete an item, select the Cut tool, and then tap the character or shape you want to delete.
	Camera	If you want to add a photo to your background or character, tap the Camera tool, and then tap the area or shape that you want to put the picture in. Then tap the Camera button to take a picture. Your picture will fill only the area or shape you selected.
	Fill	To color an object, select the Fill tool, choose a color, and then tap the area you want to fill with that color.

INDEX

RESOURCES

Visit *http://www.nostarch.com/scratchjr/* for resources, errata, and more information.

MORE SMART BOOKS FOR CURIOUS KIDS!

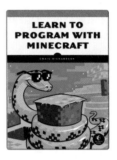